Prairie
123s

Jocey Asnong

RMB

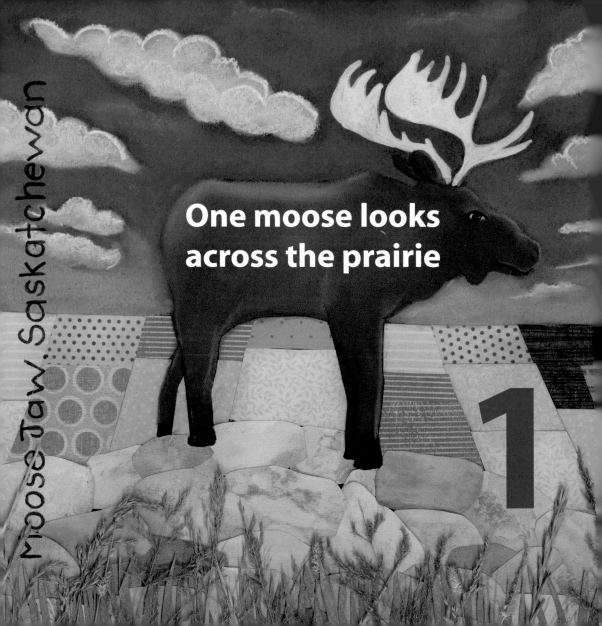

One moose looks
across the prairie

Moose Jaw, Saskatchewan

1

2

Two rodeo athletes show off their skills

Calgary, Alberta

Three squirrels
skate under
bright shiny stars

Winnipeg, Manitoba

3

4

Four lizards lounge on sun baked rocks

Medicine Hat, Alberta

Brandon, Manitoba

**Five dragonflies
dive through
the sky**

6

Six deer string
up colourful
winter lights

Lethbridge, Alberta

**Seven trout
swim beneath
a city bridge**

Saskatoon, Saskatchewan

7

8

**Eight owls watch
the forest floor**

Steinbach, Manitoba

Nine bison graze on prairie grasses

9

Grasslands National Park, Saskatchewan

Ten snow tubes slide down a canyon run

10

Red Deer, Alberta

11

Eleven meadowlarks sing country songs

Minnedosa, Manitoba

Twelve grasshoppers take a lunch break

Swift Current, Saskatchewan

13

Thirteen prairie skinks slither across the sand

Spirit Sands, Manitoba

14

Fourteen festival tents for us to see

Edmonton, Alberta

15

Fifteen goslings swim through a marsh

Regina Saskatchewan

16

**Sixteen apples
for our basket**

Morden, Manitoba

Seventeen beavers build a new home

17

Elk Island National Park, Alberta

18

Eighteen marshmallows roast over our campfire

Manitoba

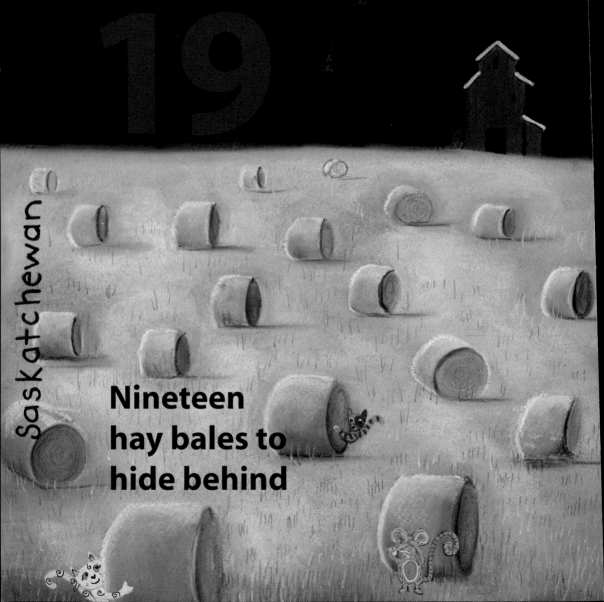

19

Saskatchewan

**Nineteen
hay bales to
hide behind**

Twenty wildflowers
sway in chinook winds

20

Alberta

JOCEY ASNONG was raised by a pack of wild pencil crayons in a house made out of paper and stories. When she is not chasing her cats around her art cave in Canmore, Alberta, she might be caught in a blizzard near Mount Everest, or running away from wolf dogs in Mongolia, or peeking out castle windows in Scotland, or sleeping under the stars in Bolivia. Jocey's books for children include *Nuptse and Lhotse Go to the Rockies* (RMB, 2014), *Nuptse and Lhotse Go to Iceland* (RMB, 2015), *Rocky Mountain ABCs* (RMB, 2016) and *Rocky Mountain 123s* (RMB, 2017).

1 2 3 4 5 6 7
8 9 10 11 12
13 14 15 16
17 18 19 20

For information on purchasing bulk quantities of this book, or to obtain media excerpts or invite the author to speak at an event, please visit rmbooks.com and select the "Contact" tab.

RMB | Rocky Mountain Books Ltd.
rmbooks.com
@rmbooks
facebook.com/rmbooks

Cataloguing data available from Library and Archives Canada
ISBN 9781771605311 (board book)
ISBN 9781771605328 (softcover)
ISBN 9781771605335 (electronic)

Printed and bound in China

We would like to also take this opportunity to acknowledge the traditional territories upon which we live and work. In Calgary, Alberta, we acknowledge the Niitsítapi (Blackfoot) and the people of the Treaty 7 region in Southern Alberta, which includes the Siksika, the Piikuni, the Kainai, the Tsuut'ina, and the Stoney Nakoda First Nations, including Chiniki, Bearpaw, and Wesley First Nations. The City of Calgary is also home to Métis Nation of Alberta, Region III. In Victoria, British Columbia, we acknowledge the traditional territories of the Lkwungen (Esquimalt and Songhees), Malahat, Pacheedaht, Scia'new, T'Sou-ke, and W̱SÁNEĆ (Pauquachin, Tsartlip, Tsawout, Tseycum) peoples.

We acknowledge the financial support of the Government of Canada through the Canada Book Fund and the Canada Council for the Arts, and of the province of British Columbia through the British Columbia Arts Council and the Book Publishing Tax Credit.

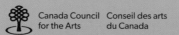